T0067184

"WATCH OUT FOR THEM BOOBY TRAPS"

AYO'

BALBOA.
PRESS

A DIVISION OF HAY HOUSE

Balboa Press books may be ordered through
booksellers or by contacting:

Balboa Press
A Division of Hay House
1663 Liberty Drive
Bloomington, IN 47403
www.balboapress.com
1 (877) 407-4847

Because of the dynamic nature of the Internet, any web
addresses or links contained in this book may have changed
since publication and may no longer be valid. The views
expressed in this work are solely those of the author and do
not necessarily reflect the views of the publisher, and the
publisher hereby disclaims any responsibility for them.

The author of this book does not dispense medical advice or prescribe
the use of any technique as a form of treatment for physical, emotional,
or medical problems without the advice of a physician, either directly
or indirectly. The intent of the author is only to offer information
of a general nature to help you in your quest for emotional and
spiritual well-being. In the event you use any of the information in
this book for yourself, which is your constitutional right, the author
and the publisher assume no responsibility for your actions.

Any people depicted in stock imagery provided by Thinkstock are
models, and such images are being used for illustrative purposes only.
Certain stock imagery © Thinkstock.

Print information available on the last page.

ISBN: 978-1-5043-7942-7 (sc)
ISBN: 978-1-5043-7943-4 (e)

Balboa Press rev. date: 07/07/2017

Dedication

My Doodlebug and Tootie Poot who taught me more than I ever dreamed about life. Doodle bug you are my outside of the box, creative, big hearted, world changer. Tootie Poot you are my talkative, insightful, don't take no for an answer, warrior. Mommy loves you both more than air!

Foreword

As a mother, even with a degree in Child and Adolescent Development, I have faced many things that humbled me. All the things I felt I knew about parenting were thrown out the window when I became a mother. Many times, I got lost in the day to day demands of motherhood and stopped celebrating my children and the joy they bring to my life.

Their struggles and life's struggles knocked me down at times but I learned to laugh instead of cry. Well sometimes I cried then laughed, and other times I cried until I laughed. My purpose in writing this book was to help other parents find the humor in life's ups and downs.

Even as I write this, I am threatening to cause bodily harm to my children if they interrupt me one more time. Don't panic they will live, me I am not so sure. Colton is rearranging my living room, which drives this OCD mom crazy. He is hiding dirty socks in my pots and pans, but no worries I will wash them before I cook with them, well if I remember. Payton is turning his comforter in to a cape and is diving off of the furniture yelling that he is taking over the world. Let's not forget the 5,000 philosophical questions he has asked today, beginning at 7am.

In the middle of this chaos it is so easy for me to forget the sweet moments. Several years ago, I decided to write down little blurbs that my boys said and funny situations that reminded me that they are precious gifts. This is what inspired me to write this book and share it with you. I want to use this to celebrate my boys, while encouraging you to do the same thing.

Acknowledgment

The journey I took to write this book began when God blessed me with two active, challenging, too smart for their own good, loving, hardheaded, creative little boys. People always say God gives the hard kids, to the parents who can handle them. I am not so sure about that but I know that I am not a bad mom, just an imperfect one who is blessed to love two little boys.

My mom and dad, who were the first people to love and believe in me. Mom, if I'm half the mom you are then I know my boys will be just fine. Dad, you instilled a drive and fire in me that nothing can extinguish. It's the VanMeter blood, I guess.

My Tribe who has supported me in raising my boys with love. Especially My Becky and Pawpaw

David. My boy's worlds were changed by you being in it.

To the man who taught me how to dream. Who pushes me to be better while loving me for the women I am. Who told me that I'm a good mom, which I love him for. Who encourages me to push past any limit I may set for myself. Keith, I love you and I will always be your Ayo'.

For my women Tribe, who has helped me grow, taught me to love me, and encouraged me to make my book a reality. I did it ladies!

Payton just asked for something to drink. I told him we had milk or water. He said, "Mom I have a question." I braced myself and asked him what it was. He said, "Mom isn't milk cow pee?" Holding back laughter I said, "No bud, not exactly."

Pawpaw was coming to pick Payton up. He texted Payton and said I am in the driveway. Payton walks by and with all seriousness he said, "Pawpaw texted and said he is in the driveway but I'm not sure if it's our driveway." He looked out the window and said, "Yea it's ours, mom, bye." I can't breathe I am laughing so hard. What driveway did he think Pawpaw was in?

Payton came in the kitchen saying, "Mom my PE teacher said to say no to drugs. I know you give me drugs so I didn't tell her because I didn't want you to get in trouble." Bless his sheltered little heart.

After a long day of working I leaned in, puckered up, and asked Colton to give me a kiss. He said, "Not with a face like that!" Well that is what rejection feels like.

Payton had made snacks for Becky and Pawpaw that he was so excited about giving them. After I read him the text they sent that said thank you he responded by saying, "Mom I really love to make them food because they really do love to eat."

After a week at Vacation Bible School Payton's teacher proudly asked him to tell me what he learned. In the silence, she asks, 'Payton who can you call on when you need something?" with a smile she waited for his answer. "Uh I don't know", he replied. "God", she said. Shaking his head, he replied, "Oh yeah I forgot His name."

Colton bit into Payton with no mercy. Payton had tears rolling down his checks as he angrily yelled, "Mom can you pray for God to take Colton to Heaven and send us a nicer baby." All I could think was at least he didn't want me to pray him to Hell.

Payton was sitting on the potty when Pawpaw David asked if he was done. Payton answered, "No not yet but Pawpaw sometimes I poop all day."

MawMaw was holding Payton and sweetly said, "Payton you are my favorite boy." Payton quickly reminded her, "I know MawMaw that is why I came to see you." Self-esteem doesn't seem to be an issue at this point.

I came to pick Payton up from Becky and Pawpaw's and when I walked onto the porch he immediately asked, "Could we stay 11 minuets?" I answered yes knowing that he really doesn't have a great concept of time. He then looked at Pawpaw and said, "You can be happy a little longer because I don't' have to leave for 11 minutes." Pawpaw said with a smile, "Being with you I am always happy." Payton quickly reminded him, "I know that is why I said that."

Payton approached me with a concerning look on his face. "Mom if you and Dad die before me can I ride my bike to MawMaw and Becky's" "Well I guess so but don't you think that could be dangerous?" I answered. He then assured me, "Mom I will ride on the grass or the sidewalk."

Sitting in a doctor's office trying to kill time I started playing a guessing game. When I said, "Payton what does a baby drinks from." He answered "A boob." I guess sometimes there are two right answers.

I was calling out math problems while Payton answered proudly. After getting three correct he was confidently sitting in his chair. When I asked, what 5 + 3 is? He answered 7. I said, "No 8 but good try." He then started to make a rewinding noise and asked me to ask the question again. After re-asking the question he said, "8. Man, I'm smart."

"Mom is Colton's name gonna be Colton when he grows up", Payton ask. "Yes" I replied. With relief in his voice he said, "Good mom because that is such a beautiful name."

Payton was out in the garden with his dad planting beans when an idea came to him. "Dad I wish I could plant Payton seeds so we could grow a bunch of Payton's." I am not sure his daddy could handle that.

Heading to the store to get Pedialight for Colton when Payton announced, "We don't need to get pedialight dad," Brandon answered, "yes we do doodle because Colton is throwing up." With an authoritative voice, Payton explained, "He won't need it dad because we prayed for him in Sunday school." Now that is childlike faith.

I was driving down the road when I heard him say, "Mom I want Becky to be my mom so I can be with her everyday." I asked him, "Well what if I miss you?" He assured me that he would come visit me.

Payton's Sunday School teacher was letting him know that this was her last Sunday because she lives too far away and it takes her too long to get to church. He inquisitively said, "You can just live with us because we live close to the church." I guess we need to start building on now.

After a long day of playing with Abigail Payton decided to end his day with one more attempt to climb to the top of Becky's tree when a loud noise startled Becky. When Becky made it to the tree there lay Payton on the ground under the tree. "Becky I should have known not to step on a dead branch."

I informed Payton that Backyardagens (his favorite TV show) goes off I will need him to clean his room. Just before the show ended he came to me and said, "Mom I am gonna go outside before Backyardegans goes off so I don't have to clean my room." Obviously in this situation honestly was not the best policy.

Sitting on the bed beside me Payton smiled as he said, "When I grow up mom I want to be a mail man so you can ride with me, because I miss you when you're not with me." That is what every mother wants to hear, but definitely not what his future wife would want.

I was getting dressed when Payton walked in. I turned my back to him just as he said, "Mom hurry put your shirt on I don't want to see your boobs." As I turned to walk away he wittily said, "Oh and watch out for those booby traps."

I was getting Colton out of the tub and slipped and fell. After making sure Colton was okay I picked him up. When I turned towards Payton he began to scream, "Oh no you knocked his pee pee off!" Holding back laughter I explained that Colton was just cold."

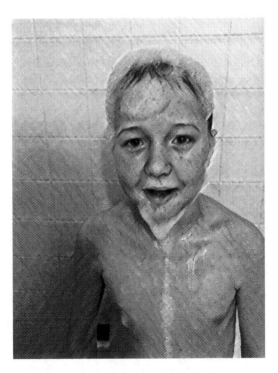

Sitting in a waiting room waiting to be seen when Payton asked, "Mom what is that?" as he pointed towards the smoke detector. I explained that it was a detector that goes off when there is smoke to warn people to get out. Before I could complete my educated answer, I was interrupted by him loudly explaining, "Oh I know mom. That is what happened when you cook." "Only when I cook toast," I replied.

With a disgusted face, Payton looked at Becky and said, "Becky your house smells like dog poop." Becky quickly answered, "No it is a diaper in the trash can." He continued to perseverate on the horrific smell that lingered in her house when she sternly said, "Payton when an adult tells you to stop saying something you stop. I have told you that it is a dirty diaper so you need to stop saying it." He turned to walk away and mumbled, "It does smell like dog poop. I am just sayin."

Pawpaw David and Payton were playing in the floor when Pawpaw stopped for a potty break. After several minutes, Payton went to the door and began to call Pawpaw. When the door opened Payton quickly informed Pawpaw that, "It does not take that long to pee." Pawpaw reluctantly informed Payton that he had to do more than pee.

I was preparing Payton for his brotherly duties by quizzing him on what babies do. I ask, "What do babies eat?" he quickly answered, "baby food". "Well what do they drink?" I asked. With great certainty, he answered, "Sweet tea." He is a true southern boy at heart.

My growing belly caught his attention. "Mom I want to talk to the baby," he announced. I started to pull my shirt up when he said, "No mom, open your mouth!" as he pulled me towards him he began to talk down my throat.

After a frustrating morning of searching for his clipboard Pawpaw decided to go ahead and leave to take Payton to school. When Pawpaw got in the truck he dialed his phone to let Mawmaw know he was leaving. Payton only seeing him dial a number intelligently said, "Pawpaw you can't call your clipboard."

After hearing the news that Payton's teacher is pregnant he quickly went to her with great news.

"Mrs. Burnette, you are gonna get big like my mom." I am sure that made her day.

Becky and I were talking about my boobs not fitting in a bathing suit. Payton said, "Mom boobs are a bad word, you shouldn't look at boobs, and you shouldn't touch boobs." Not wanting him to think boobs are this horrible thing I said, "Well Payton one day when you grow up you will get married and if your wife lets you then you can touch her boobs and look at them." He paused and asked, "Oh! Well can I kiss on them too?" With all I had in me I said, "Yes Payton if you wife lets you then you can."

Payton was sitting with Pawpaw David and let a poot slip. Pawpaw was covering his nose when Payton in a strong southern accent says, "Excuse me I'm passing the gas."

Standing in the middle of a restaurant Payton proclaimed, "Mom today when I burp it smells bad to myself." Some things just leave you speechless.

Riding to school pawpaw asked Payton what he wanted to pray about. Payton said, "Oh Pawpaw you pray I am just too tired."

Payton asked, "Mom why are your legs so bumpy in the back." I explained that it was cellulite. He walked away with a concerned face repeating the word cellulite. Poor guy probably though I was dying of something.

Payton was riding to the store with Pawpaw David and it was hot outside. Pawpaw complained about the heat when Payton assured him not to worry because he had asked God to turn the heat off.

I was lying in bed with Payton I told him that God knows the number of hairs on his head and everything he feels and thinks. He said, "Mom I know what I think too because I am the one thinking it." He is the master of the obvious.

Payton yelled from the bathroom, "Mom I am done please hurry and wipe my butt. It itches and I can't scratch it because I will get stinky on my hands." Little boys can be so graphic.

I asked Payton to put his brother diaper bag in his room. I heard him throw it and take off running. He said, "Sorry mom but I was dark frightened."

After starting a round of antibiotics, I became very sick. I had to pull over to throw up on my way to Payton's dentist app. He was so sweet. He said, "Mom I wish God didn't build you so you could get sick." I told him that God built us perfect but Adam and Eve sinned when they ate the apple God told them not to and that's why we get sick. He said, "Mom you didn't eat the apple so that's not fair." Again, I was left speechless.

Payton was eating pancakes in his underwear this morning. He looked at me stuck his chest out and said, "Mom I got syrup on my nipple." I tried not to laugh and told him to wipe it off and he said, "Nipple is a funny word huh?" It really is a funny word.

I always pray with Payton on his way to school. This morning he said mom I want to pray. "Of course," I said "go ahead." "Dear Lord, thank you

for the whole world. I think that covers it. Amen"
Yeah that definitely covers it.

Payton was getting out of the tub and said,
"Mom hurry, hurry, put my robe on me!!!! I am not
fast, wait I can run fast, never mind I'll put it on"
Glad I could be a sounding board for him to talk
that through.

Payton just informed me that the reason our
living room TV is faster (ahead by a few seconds)
because we didn't plug them in at the same time.
Makes sense to me.

After praying with Payton this morning, he
asked why I prayed that he would love Jesus
because he already does. I said because I want you
to love him even more. I proceeded to try to use
this as a teachable moment. I said you will learn
to love him more by praying and reading the bible.
You can pray anytime and about anything. You
can pray when your happy, sad, scared, anytime.
"But Mom can He hear me if I whisper because I
am supposed to whisper when I'm at school?" Yes,
He can.

Payton informed Pawpaw that he knew why he built his shop near his school. He said, "Pawpaw I know you built your shop near my school because you miss me and you will be close to me but why else did you build it here." That is a boy who knows the world rotates around him

"Mom I have an idea. We should get paper and write letters to everyone we know and love and make sure they are invited to the party at our house. We can have cake and candy. It can be after school tomorrow." Well I guess we are having a party I didn't know about.

After noticing Payton was staring at my chest in deep thought. He says, "Mom why do you have a boob crack?" I explained that it was called cleavage. He then said, "Do you have it because boys always want to look at it?" Not sure if that's its main purpose.

I woke up and went to get Colton out of the bed. When I got to his room he was not in bed. I immediately thought he must be in the living room or in Payton's room. After realizing he was not there panic set in. My heart started racing and I began running through the house. I turned the corner in his room and out of the corner of my eye I saw him. Only my child gets out of the bed in the middle of the night to sleep on his changing table. Did I forget to mention I now have several additional gray hairs?

I was loading the van this morning and fell up the stairs. Payton runs out and yells, "I know what to do." He then returns with an ice cold sopping wet washcloth and said clean the blood off. Then when I managed to hobble in the house there were Band-Aids waiting for me on the table. Now that's love.

I walked outside to get something out if the van. Payton runs after me yelling, "Mom you are supposed to keep an eye on us. We are only kids!" Oh no his next call will be DSS.

I hear a loud voice from the bathroom, "Mom hurry come look." He pointed at toilet and said, "I didn't waste a drop." I busted out laughing and said, "thank you Payton you can flush it now."

All the kids were running around playing with water guns but Payton had decided he didn't want to play. He became upset when Jazzy started spraying him. I said, "Doodle, jazzy is a baby she doesn't understand." He quickly corrected me, "Yes she does, she can talk. Babies can't talk." I guess I have been told.

My son just asked could we make Max (from Max and Ruby) our second baby brother because

Ruby is mean. He paused with such a serious face and said "I would let Max wear overalls to the pajama party." He takes those cartoons seriously.

I asked Payton if his teacher Mrs. Burnette liked her Christmas present we had made her. He answered with an annoyed voice, "Yes mom, of course, she didn't give it back." I guess that is a good indication that someone likes something.

After eating multiple snacks Pawpaw informed Payton that he could not give him another snack or his mama would kill him. After about five minutes Payton returned and said, "Pawpaw mama is going to have to kill you because I need another snack" I guess when it comes down to it food wins out.

Becky and Pawpaw watched the boys while Brandon and I went out to dinner. When I got home Payton told me he needed to tell me something. With such a sincere face he said, "Mom you work so hard to keep this house clean and Becky comes and messes it up." I have trained him well.

After watching Payton write I LOVE YOU incorrectly multiple times I said, "Payton why do you put a "y" after "I" when you write I love you. He said, "Because it's Iya love you." Poor guy was definitely raised in the south.

I pulled an empty bag of chips out of the cabinet. With disappointment, I asked Payton why he ate all the potato chips. He sweetly replied, "Mom I know they are not good for you so I ate them so you wouldn't." What a little martyr.

Colton walked by, but I could tell something was making him uncomfortable. That's when I noticed he had bulges in his footie PJ's. As I unzipped his PJ's, I found a toy car, blocks, a remote control, socks, ink pens, and a toy tire. After searching to make sure I had gotten all his hidden treasures, Colton looked up and with relief said, "Oh thanks mom." Glad I could help, I thought.

You know women can be emotional at times. Well this morning was one of those mornings. I was crying when Payton walked in and he asked what's wrong. I told him I was just really happy. He looked at me with the strangest face and said, "mom you only cry when you're sad. I already told you that a while back." He walked away and I'm sure he was thinking, dang women are crazy.

My dad was late picking Payton up from school. When Payton got in his truck he said, "this thing with you being late calls for a special meeting of the brotherhood." I don't know about you, but I'm worried about my dad. That doesn't sound good at all.

My stomach has been upset all day so I have spent most of my day in the bathroom. Payton came home and I asked for a hug. He went to walk towards me and then stopped in his tracks. "Do you still have diarrhea?" Man, the poops will stop some loving really quick.

My son informed me that he loved me because I am smart. When I said, "well don't you think mommy is pretty too?" He paused and answered "No". Well I guess I shouldn't ask if I don't want to know.

Payton asked me if I needed help carrying groceries. I said yes so, he hands me a picture where he had traced his hands and said, "Here have a hand". Oh, I guess somebody is full of himself today.

Driving home today we passed a local church cometary. Payton said, "Mom I don't EVER want to go to that church. Look everyone dies that goes there!" I'm dying. No pun intended.

We were driving home when Payton said, "look mom." I said, "I can't look doodle I'm driving." He said, "Mom why can't you look while you're driving if you have eyes in the back of your head." Shoot my cover is busted.

I had asked Payton to go start the car. He said, "Okay, I need to pee!". "well go pee", I replied. "Mom I NEED TO PEE!" I yelled back, "GO PEE!!!!!" I saw him take a deep breath and he said, "I don't need to pee. I need the keys". I said, "Oh sorry. Here you go." As he walked away he mumbled to Colton, "Man she really needs to start listening."

Colton was sitting on the porch with his cousin who was telling him all about Jesus. She said, "You can ask him in your and heart." He quickly replied, "But my tummy is in there!" Valid point Nicodemus Jr.

Payton asked me why do we have spiders. Of course, since I am such a good mom, I decided to make this conversation a science lesson on nature.

"Well bud they help keep other bugs from over populating.", I said sharing all my vast knowledge on insects. With a confused look, he said, "what is over populating?" I continued to explain, "It's when there is too many of a certain bug or animal." I saw the light bulb cut on above his head, "Oh I get it. Is that like when Mawmaw says she can't handle all of us (AKA all her grandkids) because we are over populating?" I know that is not exactly right, but my vast knowledge had run out so I said yes. Don't judge.

I was watching a drug intervention show with Payton. I thought it's never too early to start talking about drugs. I said, "Doodle do you know what drugs are?" He confidently replied, "of course mom I know what drugs is. You know it's like I drug my book bag on the floor." Well I didn't accomplish my goal, but at least I don't have to worry about him using anytime soon.

I was finishing up the kitchen after dinner and yes the boys were supposed to be in bed. Colton comes in the kitchen with his hand on his hips and said, "Mom I want to sleep with Payton but he said no so you need to make him do chores because that is ugly." I guess I have been told.

I was displaying my mothering skills while at Payton's school for a Spring festival. Of course, it's not a festival without a grape ice'. After finishing the yummy icee I asked Payton, "Is mommy's teeth purple?" He bluntly answered, "No mom they are still yellow." I forgive you nice lady who was standing behind me that hysterically laughed tears, because I have to admit it was funny.

I have failed as a mother. My 2-year-old just walked in and said, "Mom get up and go in the kitchen". I guess he is hungry and I should know my role.

I was trying to work from home but it was not very successful. Colton came in and laid the recliner back. I said, "Tootie I can't work like this." He said, "Well mom when you need to reach one of those square buttons then call me." "Colton! Colton! Colton!" Well he disappeared.

Payton kept saying boob over and over. I said, "if you say boob again I am gonna go into the other room because you don't talk like that around a lady." He paused, looked me in my face and said, "nipple." When I cut my eyes at him, he smiled and said, "I didn't say boob." He isn't even a teenager yet. Jesus help me.

Colton saw me working out in my sports bra. He looked at me in utter disgust and said, "why are you only wearing your boob holder." I'm not sure if it was the fact that I was running on the elliptical or not but I have no words.

I was taking Colton into daycare today. I asked if he was ready to go. He said, "hold on" then licked his hand and laid his hair down. Well I guess he is ready now.

Picking Colton up from Ms. Karla's and I asked how he behaved. She said he needed to work on listening. I squatted down and said, "Tootie are you listening to Ms. Karla?" He put his finger over his mouth and said, "Shhhh mom Mich is sleeping. You can't talk." He is an expert at dodging a question.

Payton was walking in the house when he started yelling, "hurry mom the wind is blowing so hard its moving the moon. See it just went behind those clouds!" I knew he was wrong, so why did I run?

I was getting Payton out of the tub and he said, "mom you know I can pee in the tub because it just turns into water. I pee and it's yellow then the yellow goes away. That's it turning into water." Please remind me never to take a bath with him.

My three-year-old just came in my room and said, "I love you mom." I said, "oh Tootie I love you too." I'm a woman so of course I couldn't stop there. I said, "Why do you love me?" He was so excited to answer, "because you have a flat butt. I love flat butts." I just added something to my things to do list. Yep Squats.

After picking Colton up from Day Care He began to tell me what for. "Mom it's not a good idea to leave me and not ask first. I was really berry upset because you leave me. You have to say please can I leave you Colton. That's what you do. Okay?" I guess I need to sit down with my supervisor and let them know I may be missing some days in the near future.

Payton always loves to asked question at 7am in the morning. "Mom why is Mr. Potato Head called Mr. Potato Head when his head isn't the only things that is a potato?" It was just too early so I said, "I don't know Payton but that's a good point."

Colton was outside playing when he said, "mom you know what? I hope to be a bicycle one day." I said, "you mean you want a bike?" He sternly replied, "no mom! I am gonna be a bicycle!!!!!" I said with my motivational voice, "Ok bud you can be anything you want to be."

Payton had a friend over for a super bowl party. I just heard him say, "Here Colton I'm giving you a piece of gum because you are doing a great job leaving me and Ryan alone." As Payton went back in his room I heard him tell Ryan, "I gave him a reward. My mom does that and it helps. "The struggles of being a big brother is real.

Payton had spent the night with Becky so I sent him a picture of my lips puckered up and texted here's a kiss from your mom. Becky said when he opened the picture he yelled, "Jehumpin ja hosafat!" He thinks he is funny.

I was cleaning out the car when the wind blew the door and it shut on my leg. I screamed in pain. Payton ran outside to find me crying, "I want my mama!" That poor child looked panicked. I know he was thinking, oh no you are the mom, so what do I do.

Colton and I went to Bojangles before getting Payton and I couldn't resist the Bo-rounds. I handed one back to him and he looked at it crazy and said, "mom are you sure about this?" I thought oh yes, I am positive. If you don't want it, I will be more than willing to eat yours.

My sweet child walked into the room upset. He was worried that there may be dead people that might have an itch, but they can't scratch it until heaven. Some conversations don't need a response. This was one of those.

Four-year-old Colton and my bestie deb were getting into my mom's car. Colton said, "Deb it was blurry and I couldn't see you. I thought it was a puppy." Deb said "she guess's it's time for her to start pulling her hair back."

Today was Payton's first basketball game of the season. He was so excited and rushing me. He said, "Mom we need to go now!" I was not quite ready so I said, "Well do you want me to go in my bra?" He said, "Yeah and all the other mom's will be jealous." I appreciated his compliment, but I didn't take the risk of testing his theory.

Payton showed his southern root today. "Mom on Peppa Pig they call a buggy a trolley. Everyone knows it's a buggy", he said with a giggle. I felt compelled to educate him on the fact that it is actually called a shopping cart. I said, "Bud it's actually called a shopping cart, but we call it a buggy." With a confused looked he asked, "Why?" I said, "Probably because shopping cart takes too long to say." He said, "Oh yeah probably." I'm glad we ironed that out.

Payton was watching TV when he said, "mom that commercial didn't make sense." I asked why. He said, "Because they said a hand full of people and people don't fit in a hand." I tried to explain a figure of speech. "Doodle what he means is that it's just a few people." "Well people should say what they mean.", he demanded. He is smarter than he knows.

I was giving Payton a bath and trying to wash his hair when he informed me that I needed to hurry because I was wasting his bath time washing him. I guess a bath serves a different purpose for a 5-year-old boy.

Payton had drunk an entire slurpy and immediately asked for another. I told him that one was enough, but then the debate started, "But mom you saw that after I drank the slurpy I gave daddy a blanky, so slurpy's are good for me because they make me do nice stuff."

After getting the boys dressed I said, "wow you two are handsome. Daddy and I made some cute kids." Payton quickly asked, "How did you make us?" I quickly replied, "I meant God made you." Whew I am not ready for that conversation.

My three-year-old is a true business man. He was standing on my computer bag, so I asked him to get off. He stood tall and stuck out hand. With the most serious look he said, "you want me to move then give me coins." I did not give him coins but, I couldn't help but laugh.

Payton started my day off with a bang. "Mom your belly sticks out like you have a baby." I said, "well bud that's because when mommy's belly's grow it doesn't go back like it looked before, but that's okay. It happens to mommies sometimes." Then he said, "well it looks pretty on you mom." I said, "aww thanks bud." But before I could digest my compliment he was crying. When I asked, what was wrong he said, "I lied mom. I don't think it looks pretty." Well I might be chunky, but I raised an honest child.

Payton was watching Tarzan. He said, "Mom I can't believe parents let Tarzan be a kid show." I said, "why?" He said, "Because he is in his underwear in front of a girl he doesn't know." He makes a good point. Come on parents you should know better.

Payton was drawing a portrait of Colton, so he was telling him to stand very still. Colton said, "Oh Payton, can you draw me a mustache and diaper and a belt and me will look just like daddy." I am a little confused about diaper but to each his own.

Colton was eating a snack while wearing an oversized shirt. He looked so cute I told him to say cheese. I was going to take his picture but he started to cry. I asked him why he was crying and he said, "don't take my cheese." Oh poor guy thought I was going to take his snack and he is serious about his dairy.

At Walmart, the cashier was wearing very creative makeup. Thick painted on eyebrows with dark purple and blue eye shadow. Payton said, "mom look at her." I immediately thought oh sweet

Jesus please make him mute. Then he said, "mom you should do your eyes like that. She is beautiful." Those are the moments when you know God hears your prayers.

Payton was talking to Becky bragging about how far he can jump. He said, "I jumped far. I jumped over the other jump." I am not sure what that means but it sounds like an accomplishment to me.

Payton was having a play date with Ryan when I overheard him talking to Ryan. "Ryan, you know what I have thought about all day?" Ryan asked what. Payton said, "They say Winnie the pooh. Like Winnie the alligator but Pooh isn't an animal. I mean what's a pooh?" Ryan just stood there blinking. I think he felt that Payton was being a little too deep.

Colton was at the pool with Mawmaw and he asked her to eat his toes. She opened wide and took a bite. He looked at her and said, "taste like chicken." He is so full of himself.

Colton kept asking for more Sprite but he had not finished what he had. I kept saying, "no you haven't drunk what you have yet." He then turned to Payton and asked. Payton answered with an adult voice, "no sir. I would have to agree with mom on this one." Well they say parents should have a unified front. I guess that applies to brothers too.

Payton and I were watching a wedding show. I said, "wow the bride is beautiful." Payton said, "then why did he call her phenomenal?" I said, "because phenomenal means amazing or gorgeous." He said, "Oh I thought that was like the phenomenal snowman." I fought back laughter and said, "No bud that's the Abominable Snowman not the Phenomenal Snowman." On his defense they do sound a lot alike.

Colton got out of bed for the hundredths time. He said that he was hungry. Did I tell you that he didn't eat the dinner I cooked? Well he didn't so I said, "Dinner time is over." He left and came back with his computer. He set his computer up and said, "I'm looking up dinner time." Wait for it........ "No mom it's still dinner time." Well who can argue with google.

During Payton's basketball practice Colton approached his coach and said, "I'm watching my brother play." His coach said, "Oh okay. I can tell he is your brother." Colton shoot back, "Yeah we have the same faces but different shirts."

In the middle of my shower my water stopped. Yep I was covered in bubbles. Colton was determined to convince me that a ghost came in and stole our water. I am trying to make phone calls to see if anyone in the area has water, but I can't hear over him singing "I ain't afraid of no ghost." If Colton is right, I'm going to need the ghost to bring my water back.

I was texting Payton while he was in the other room. I just set his tablet up so I can use my email and send him text. His first text said, "I got all your apps mom" and I said, "I love you, doodlebug." He came into my room and said, "Mom can we have one conversation. Like, I text you a topic and you text me the same topic back. I texted you about apps and you said I love you, doodlebug, which is two topics." Forgive me small child, I was being a girl.

Colton woke me up at 5:30am, on a Saturday. He kept saying he was hungry but he didn't want to go in the kitchen because he was afraid of the dark. I said, "Mommy isn't getting up right now, it's too early." About 30 mins later I noticed a strange light and got up to figure out what it was. I came in to find Colton sitting on his bed in a diaper, wearing a forehead light, eating a Hunnybun. What can I say, this kid is going places?

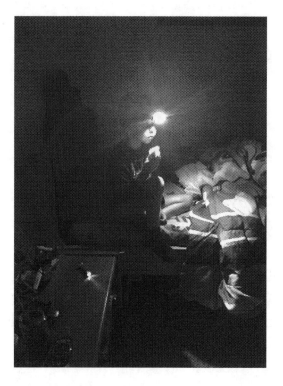

Colton was reading his Bible and said that God had a secret and for me to come listen. I was so excited that he had heard from God. Then he spoke, "Mom, God really doesn't love everyone". After arguing with him I decided to let it go. Later a perfect opportunity arose when he was playing with his new globe. "Colton can you believe God built the whole world!", I said with a hopeful heart. "Well it wasn't hard mom! Jesus helped.", he said with a 5 going on 15 voice. Well dang I am 2:0.